Wags and Kisses

A *For Better or For Worse*® Little Book

By Lynn Johnston

Andrews McMeel Publishing

Kansas City

For information, write
Andrews McMeel Publishing,
an Andrews McMeel Universal company,
4520 Main Street, Kansas City, Missouri 64111.

ISBN: 0-7407-1453-8

Poem by Andie Parton

You don't really want a pet
Think of visits to the vet

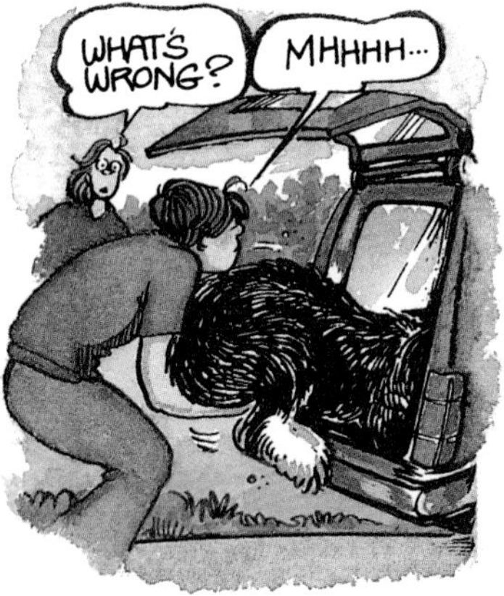
WHAT'S WRONG?
MHHHH...

Fleas and fur balls everywhere
Chewed-up toys and underwear

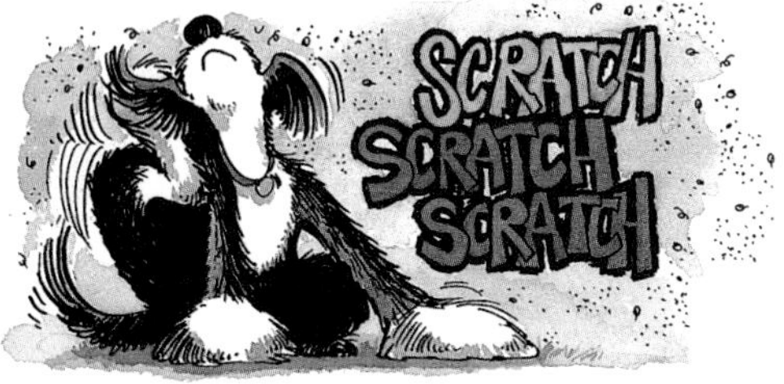
SCRATCH
SCRATCH
SCRATCH

Then you see a puppy—wait
You're in love and it's too late

Licks your face and wags his tail
You resist, to no avail
(You're in luck, 'cause he's for sale!)

Bring him home, he's so much fun
Loves to nap and eat and run

Harmless pup, no sense of doom
Turn your back, he'll trash the room

Mangled chairs and chewed-up boots
Shredded phone books, tattered suits

Mournful eyes with baleful looks
Just can't stay in your bad books

He will slobber, drool, and beg
Snore and belch and date your leg

Short on manners, long on charm
Just a doggie, what's the harm?

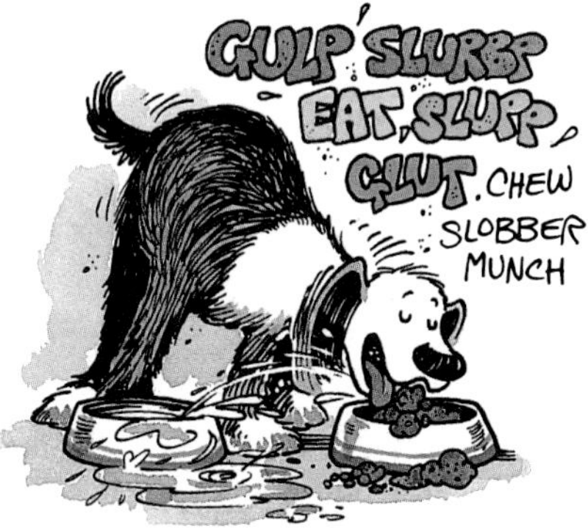
GULP SLURRP
EAT SLURP
GLUT CHEW
SLOBBER
MUNCH

The forbidden antique bed
Where he likes to lay his head

When he thinks no one's around
So surprised when he is found

Wags his tail without remorse
Thinks he owns the place, of course

He won't heel, or fetch a stick
Won't obey, and has no tricks

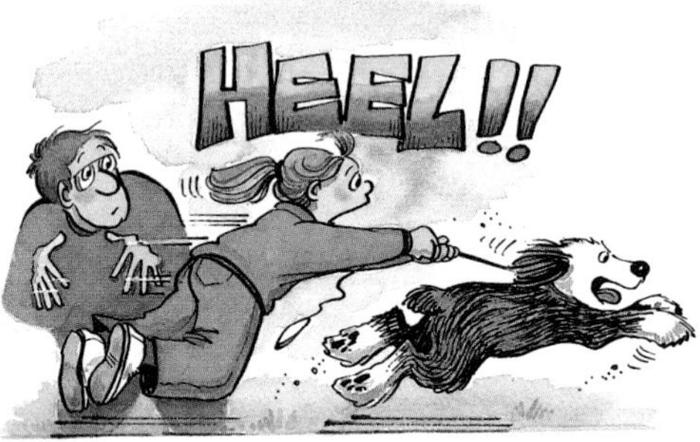
HEEL!!

No he isn't very smart
But you knew that from the start

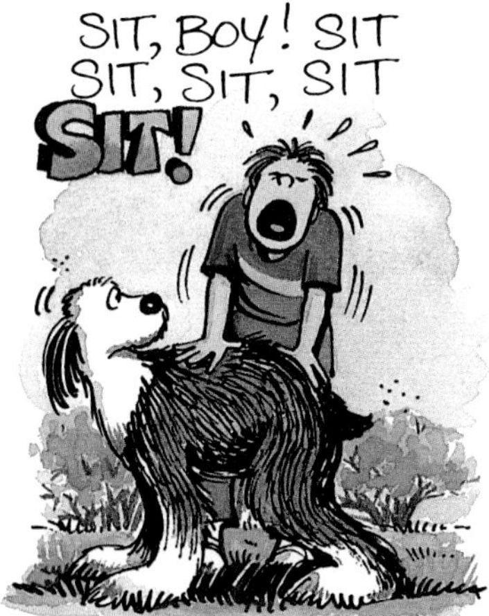
SIT, BOY! SIT
SIT, SIT, SIT
SIT!

Yet who's walking with the scoop
Bagging up the doggie poop?

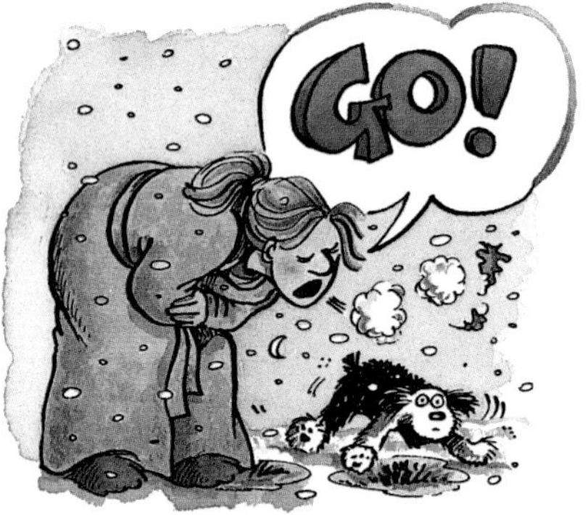
GO!

Garbage is a dog's delight
Road kill is a favorite sight

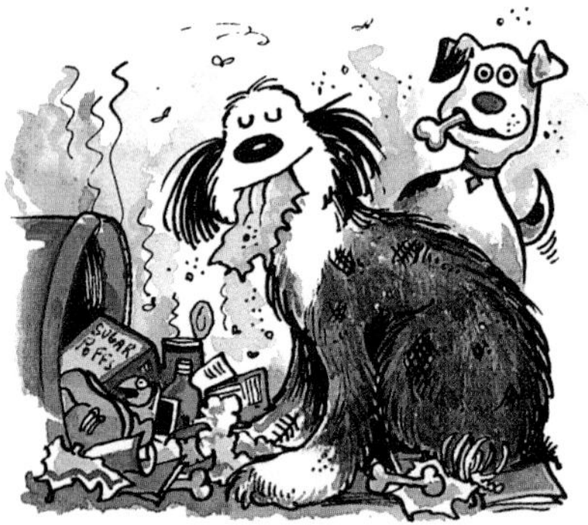
SUGAR
PUFFS

Twitchy dreams of trash abound
Gourmet heaven for your hound

Puddles 'neath the neighbors' tree
Can't pretend you didn't see

Prowling through the neighborhood
Stealing toys and firewood

Stolen goods to be returned
More dog lessons to be learned

Is he Daddy's poochie poo?
Izzie Mummy's pupperoo?

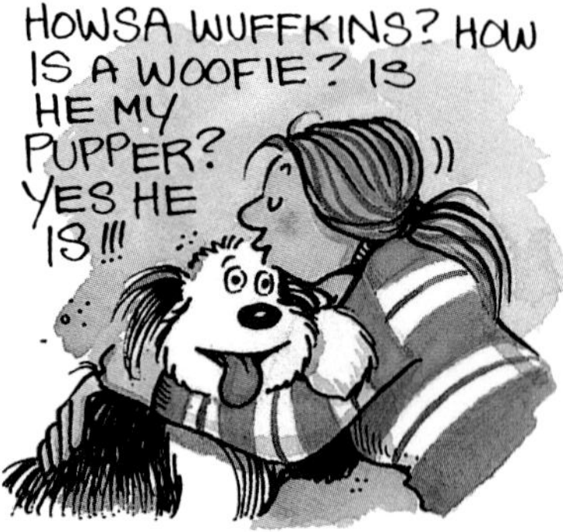
HOWSA WUFFKINS? HOW IS A WOOFIE? IS HE MY PUPPER? YES HE IS!!!

Baby talk, let no one know
Laughingstock of friend and foe

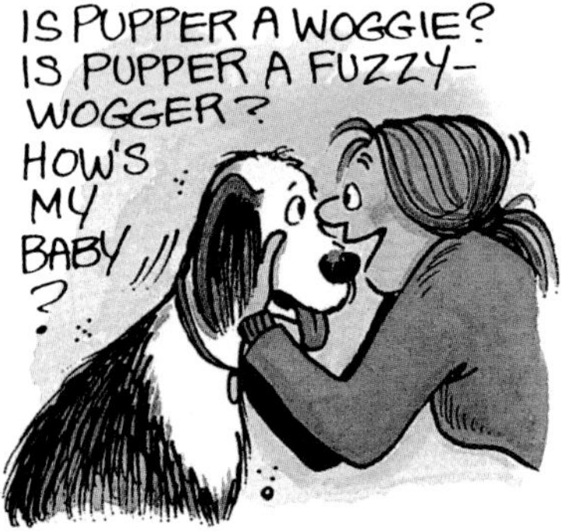
IS PUPPER A WOGGIE?
IS PUPPER A FUZZY-WOGGER?
HOW'S MY BABY?

Life is hard, come home and play
Get your fur fix every day

Sloppy greetings at the door
Who could ever love you more?

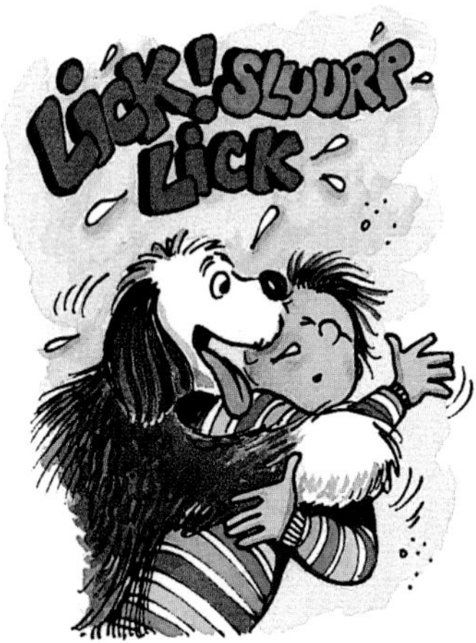
LICK! SLUURP
LICK

Always knows just when you're blue
Snuggles up to comfort you

You could have bad hair, bad breath
Be hungover, look like death

You may not be cool or smart
But a dog sees from the heart

To your dog you're God above
No conditions to his love

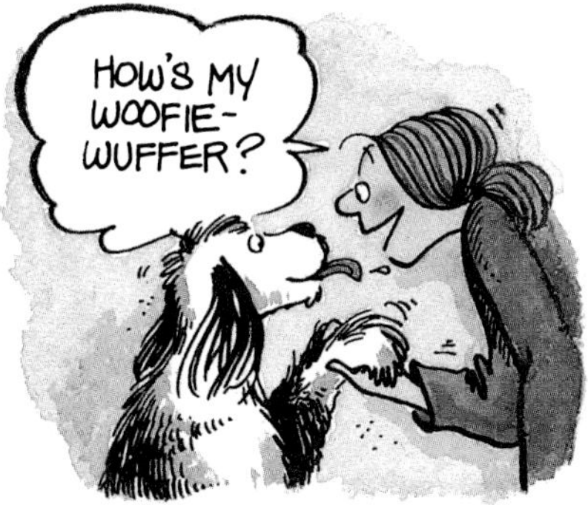
HOW'S MY WOOFIE-WUFFER?

Underfoot and in the way?

No, he's family, and here to stay.